A Walk Through Forgiveness

Bob Lively

DIMENSIONS
FOR LIVING
NASHVILLE

A WALK WITH GOD THROUGH FORGIVENESS

Copyright © 2005 by Bob Lively

All rights reserved.

This book is printed on recycled, acid-free, elemental-chlorine–free paper.

ISBN 0-687-05502-4

Library of Congress Control Number: 2005924154

Scripture quotations unless otherwise noted are from the Revised Standard Version of the Bible copyright 1946, 1952 by the Division of Christian Education of the National Council of the Churches of Christ in the United States of America. Used by permission.

Scripture quotations noted NASB are from the New American Standard Bible © copyright The Lockman Foundation 1960, 1962, 1963, 1968, 1971, 1972, 1973, 1975, 1977, 1995. Used by permission.

Scripture quotations noted NRSV are from the New Revised Standard Version of the Bible, copyrighted © 1989 by the Division of Christian Education of the National Council of the Churches of Christ in the United States of America, and are used by permission.

05 06 07 08 09 10 11 12 13 14 — 10 9 8 7 6 5 4 3 2 1

MANUFACTURED IN THE UNITED STATES OF AMERICA

Grudges

For thou, O Lord, art good and forgiving, / abounding in steadfast love to all who call on thee. **(Psalm 86:5)**

The shack keeps its silent vigil, just as it has done for close to a century on a road older than even the fledgling Republic of Texas. Today it is smothered by kudzu vine that has morphed it into the shape of a long-ago abandoned haystack as it casts a broad shadow on the dirt redder than the inside of a watermelon. When I was young, it was a mom-and-pop grocery, and its proprietors were the village mayor and his wife. For some now-forgotten reason, the adults in our family decided that these folks had wronged us. Punishment was definitely intended by our decision to quit buying light bread from them, which meant we had to drive twelve miles one way to buy it from someone else.

All the folks involved in that silly dispute are now gone from this life, but the old shack and the memories it stirs up indict me as I recall the small bit of satisfaction I found in taking sides and in believing that vengeance was justified.

Lord God, I know that grudges are nothing more than a big, toxic clump of infected anger, yet I hold tighter to them than ever to money. Grant me the courage to let go. Amen.

Absolution

For I am sure that neither death, nor life, . . . nor things present, nor things to come, nor powers, nor height, nor depth, nor anything else in all creation, will be able to separate us from the love of God in Christ Jesus our Lord. (Romans 8:38-39)

—⚍—

Her pain was so intense as to appear inconsolable. I listened but said nothing, although I wanted to ease her suffering. To attempt a rescue would only make things worse, so I remained silent while not taking my eyes from her. She leaned forward and began coughing so violently, I feared she might pass out. I placed my hands gently upon her shoulders, and she raised her eyes to meet my concern and cried before she said, "I killed a baby twenty-five years ago. It was my baby! I had an abortion! I can't believe that I can be forgiven. I am so guilty and so filled with shame. I am so terrible!"

I took her by the hand, and she and I walked with other members of our group to a lake across the street. There, I handed her a stone. "What's this?" she asked, still trembling. "Your burden," I answered. "Hurl it into the lake and watch the water absorb it." She accepted the invitation. Once the splash was done, I hugged her and whispered, "God forgives you absolutely." I would never see her again, but she wrote to say that in our moment together she had been struck by grace.

Lord God, why is it that we're so brutally hard on ourselves? Amen.

Trust

Likewise the Spirit helps us in our weakness; for we do not know how to pray as we ought, but the Spirit himself intercedes for us with sighs too deep for words. (**Romans 8:26**)

—∞—

I asked myself if there was anyone I could not forgive. The answer that greeted me quicker than a hiccup was a loud *Yes!* I realized I could forgive, but I didn't want to. I decided that there must be a very fine line between desire and decision. If I worked for several years at the attempt to will my broken heart to forgive the individual who so slandered me once upon a time, I might be successful. But the fact is that I will never forget. How can I? My mind is hardwired for memory. This forgive-and-forget business is myth.

So what do I do? The solution lies in trusting Jesus. So I asked Jesus to forgive me for not being willing to forgive the man who hurt me, and later I found the courage to let go of this wrong. I cannot do for myself the hard work that forgiveness requires. Honestly, I'm not wise enough to know even where to begin. But from this most recent in-depth effort at forgiveness, I have come to believe that sincerely wanting to forgive is probably all that is required of us. God takes it from there.

We find it so difficult to trust you, O God. We say that we do, but we behave in ways that betray our words. Amen.

Grace

There is therefore now no condemnation for those who are in Christ Jesus. (**Romans 8:1**)

—⁂—

Nick and Nancy, Uncle Will's two big plow horses, began to turn their ears as if a thunderstorm might be brewing, but the late-February sky was as clean as mopped hardwood. Uncle Will halted the animals, rested the guide strap upon the handles, and ambled to the barbed-wire fence, where he glimpsed a chain gang slinking down the old road.

A horseman sounded a whistle and ordered the chained men to rest. All but one fell to the dirt. The lone standing prisoner glared at Uncle Will in stony silence. Uncle Will had long believed that all human beings, regardless of their circumstances, were deserving of respect and expressions of kindness simply because God is love. But perhaps put off by this plowman's curiosity, the prisoner requested the absurd. "Play me a fiddle tune, mister."

Uncle Will trotted to the house, lifted his prized fiddle from a shelf in a closet, and returned to the road before the chained men were ordered to move. And across that taut strand of barbed wire that momentarily separated freedom from bondage and promise from despair, Uncle Will pulled from the strings of his fiddle his favorite old hymn, "Amazing Grace." When he was finished, the man on the horse blew his whistle, and every man in chains who passed by spoke a word of gratitude to the man who held the fiddle and wore a grin.

Lord God, allow your grace to stretch our compassion beyond the barriers. Amen.

Making Amends

I will be as the dew to Israel; / he shall blossom as the lily, / he shall strike root as the poplar; / his shoots shall spread out; / his beauty shall be like the olive, / and his fragrance like Lebanon. **(Hosea 14:5-6)**

—⁓—

Recovering alcoholics know that apologies are meaningless. Resorting to an apology likely means we have failed to recognize the depth of the pain we caused. People who are conscious don't make apologies; they make amends. So what is the difference? Making amends plows much deeper and serves to keep us conscious. When we make an amend, we say:

I recognize I injured you.
I regret that I hurt you.
I hurt you because I was not conscious at the time.
I promise never to do this again.

Making amends to God is the discipline of confession, and this is important because we will never know that we are forgiven until we accept responsibility for what we have done.

God, inspire in us the courage to make amends. Amen.

From the Mouths of Babes

"Out of the mouth of babes and sucklings thou hast brought perfect praise." (**Matthew 21:16**)

—∿—

She was only three when I lifted her to the old hackberry stump. This was her first visit to the red land where my roots run deep, and I wanted to see her atop the old stump where as a boy I often flung my granddaddy's saddle so that I might chase outlaws. She raised her arms, and I rested her on the surface worn smooth by more than a century of weather. I then took a step backward so I could focus the camera. Suddenly, she shrieked and ripped at her tiny shirt.

"Fants! Daddy! Fants!"

Dropping the camera, I lunged to liberate her from the angry fire ants. Before I could brush them away, she'd been stung at least thirty times. Minutes later her great-grandmother rubbed on her wounds a soothing homemade remedy composed of well water and baking soda. I stood above where she lay and wept. Sensing my anguish, my three-year-old looked at me through her teary eyes and said, "It's OK, Daddy. You didn't mean to."

Teach us to listen, O Lord, to the wisdom that comes to us from children. Amen.

The Sacrament of Supper

And he took bread, and when he had given thanks he broke it and gave it to them, saying, "This is my body." **(Luke 22:19)**

—⁓—

Uncle Will's prized possession was a fiberglass fishing rod, and, unwittingly, I destroyed it. Although I was only five, I was still old enough to scheme.

When Uncle Will announced it was time to go home for supper, I reeled in the line on my cane pole and dashed to the car where I planned to ride in the front seat. I'd ridden all the way to the muddy banks of Pedro Creek in the backseat, where I choked on road dust. Uncle Will and I arrived at the front seat at the same time, one step ahead of my brother. I yanked open the door and slammed it hard, only to witness Uncle Will's glass rod cut into two halves. He pulled open the door, sighed deeply, and said, "Bobby, I sure wish you hadn't done that." He then said, "Well, let's go home to supper." And that evening he smiled at me as he passed me a plate full of my grandmother's home cooking and said, "Here, take, eat, this is for you."

We give thanks, Lord, that we learn to forgive by first being forgiven. Amen.

Shame

"And forgive us our debts, / As we also have forgiven our debtors."
(Matthew 6:12)

—⚊—

Shame is an eclipse casting a dark shadow upon one's core truth. Further, this insidious force is birthed by the always erroneous conviction that we are terribly flawed and should feel bad about who we are. Shame, then, invites us to believe false messages regarding our personal worth rather than to embrace the truth that we have been created in the image of God and that every human being is an expression of the Creator's highest thought.

Grace is the only power strong enough to exorcise the cruel demon that is shame. Furthermore, grace is always the truth, while shame is the harbinger of lies and the author of toxic ideation. In the wake of the soul's courageous willingness to forgive, shame lifts like an autumn fog, and for just a while a soul is blessed with the amazing gift of clarity. Grace draws the restored soul so close to God that it sees what the eye never can. And in that pristine moment we see anger and grudges for what they are—well-crafted expressions of fear. All heartfelt forgiveness is a lantern, erasing from the soul's landscape every dark shadow cast by shame.

Illumine the shadows, O Lord. Amen.

Interloper

"Blessed are the merciful, for they shall obtain mercy."
(Matthew 5:7)

—⚏—

He broke into the soup-kitchen line, and I politely requested that he return to the end of the line. His stare indicated that he had no idea what I meant, so I motioned for Rico to interpret in Spanish. Rico complied, and the man trudged to the end of the line. Not fifteen minutes later he was again first in line. Once more, I approached him and had Rico explain a second time in Spanish that if he broke in line again, I would remove him from the soup kitchen. Before I could return to my work, he violated the rule a third time. Only two minutes after I paused to thank God for our daily bread, I ushered this man outside. Satisfied, I returned to the soup kitchen and served lunch to several hundred men.

An hour later, I returned to the dining room to see the little man I had treated so rudely mopping the floor. His witness stunned me; nevertheless, I did manage to whisper to God, "This man knows Jesus." He returned the smile I offered sheepishly and then followed me into the kitchen, where I prepared for both of us a lunch of beef stew and thick wedges of cornbread. We sat across the table from each other and nodded and enjoyed our daily bread as brothers in Christ.

Dear Lord, teach us that wisdom is patience. Amen.

Theft

How precious is thy steadfast love, O God! / The children of men take refuge in the shadow of thy wings. (Psalm 36:7)

—⟋⟋⟍—

I was ravenous as I tossed the *Dallas Morning News* onto more than a hundred front porches; nevertheless, this adolescent hunger was a mere excuse, not a reason, for antisocial behavior. I discovered that the bread box at Mr. Parker's store was filled with pastries as I raised the lid. I then helped myself to a half-dozen warm glazed donuts. Sitting on a curb, I rolled newspapers and washed down several purloined pastries with a soda before dumping the rest of the donuts down a storm drain.

Later I realized that I could no longer enter Mr. Parker's grocery store. The guilt I felt was powerful. I'd known Mr. and Mrs. Parker all my life, and he was consistently kind and affirming. Everything I did in the way of being recognized, he managed to hear about and praise. He'd often say, "Bobby, you're just like your daddy. Your character is impeccable." It was an honor to be compared to my father. Once the guilt became too much, I penned Mr. Parker a letter:

Dear Mr. Parker:
I stole your donuts. I put $5 I earned mowing a yard into this envelope to cover the cost. I hope it does. Please forgive me.

I dropped the unsigned letter and the five dollars in the box and never stole again.

Thank you, Lord, that grace is greater than guilt. Amen.

Mercy

O give thanks to the LORD, for he is good; / for his steadfast love endures forever. **(1 Chronicles 16:34 NRSV)**

—∿∿—

Mercy is at the center of all good spirituality. When one refuses mercy, God is rejected. The reason is simple: Mercy is God's identity. Said another way, God's essence is grace. Many people erroneously believe that Christianity is a meritocracy, where those who "get it right" are more loved by God than those who don't. Jesus saw reality differently. He first sought out those who were getting it wrong, such as the tax collectors and the prostitutes, so that he might assure them that they were both loved and forgiven. Mercy is the portal through which the grateful enter the kingdom of God. Grace, then, is the key, but it is not our key. Rather it is God's key. And God chooses to unlock the door to the Kingdom not because we've been good or lived our lives particularly well. No, God swings wide the door because God is mercy. Grace liberates us from the temptation to be proud. Also, it frees us from all unhealthy preoccupation with ourselves as it plants the seed of forgiveness deep within the rich soil of our souls. Without it, we would be lost; but because of it, we are saved. And saved people are forgiving people.

Make us sufficiently conscious to be merciful, O God. Amen.

An Old Brass Rooster

And Peter remembered the saying of Jesus, "Before the cock crows, you will deny me three times." **(Matthew 26:75)**

—m—

An old brass rooster is perched atop the steeple of a Presbyterian church in East Texas. Years ago, I inquired of a church elder as to its meaning. "The tradition is European," he informed me. "The rooster is the symbol that, like Peter, we in the church deny Christ every day. Furthermore, the brass bird is attached to a weathervane that turns the rooster always to face the wind."

I asked, "What does that signify?"

He smiled and said, "Even though we deny Christ, we still know that the gospel always goes against the world's great winds."

"How so?" I asked, not certain I got his point.

I will never forget his words: "The world is big on vengeance, while the gospel is only about one thing—grace."

Lord, keep us ever mindful of the rooster as he turns to face the wind. Amen.

Screen-Door Proclamation

It is God who justifies; who is to condemn? **(Romans 8:33b-34)**

—⚯—

A friend happened into a restaurant in a Texas border town in search of a sandwich. As he entered what he described to be an uncomfortably warm room that was stained and ripened by a century of cigar smoke, his eye glimpsed a sign affixed to the screen door. He sat at the counter and ordered the sandwich and iced tea, and did his best to soak in the atmosphere for which this one-room establishment was famous on both sides of the Rio Grande. Curiosity getting the best of him, he rose to his feet and shuffled outside once more to read this astounding proclamation contained in the small hand-lettered sign. It read:

For Members and Non-Members Only!

On his way north, he stopped in Austin to tell me about the sign. He asked, "Does this idea come from the Bible?"

I answered, "No." But about that I was wrong. It does come from Scripture, and more specifically, from Paul's letter to the church at Rome. The words are different, but the meaning is the same: "It is God who justifies; who is to condemn?"

Deliver us from the temptation to discriminate. Amen.

Cleaning Up One's Own House

"But if any one strikes you on the right cheek, turn to him the other also." (Matthew 5:39)

—∿—

I only need to clean up my own house. I'm not responsible for correcting others. But I am definitely responsible for my own stuff. Many years ago I wrote a letter of amends to a man about whom I'd said some harsh things. I said what I said because I was not yet conscious. What I could not see at the time is that what I expressed was the projection of my own unsettled interior. I once believed that this man was my problem, but about that I was wrong. *I* was my problem. Recognizing this, I asked God to restore me to a place where love might flow through me. So I wrote a letter to this man who was the former object of my projection, and I stated that I knew that I had wounded him and that I accepted full responsibility for having hurt him.

Weeks passed. Finally, I received a return letter from him that was full of his own projections directed at me. I winced, paused long enough to pray, and then I asked God to forgive both of us for our spiritual immaturity. Once I said "Amen," I was very glad that I had begun to clean up my own disordered house.

Lord, keep us focused on what it is about us that needs attention. Amen.

Struck by Grace

"Let your light so shine before men, that they may see your good works and give glory to your Father who is in heaven."
(Matthew 5:16)

—⁊⁊—

Juan was struck by grace. I have no idea how or why it happened, but I know it happened. He was knocked to the ground, and when he awakened he was dazed for some time; but even more, he was liberated from the craving for cocaine. Confused and more than a little grateful, he found a church where his story was accepted with no skepticism. Months later his adult daughter was killed when a drive-by shooter sprayed a rain of bullets into the car where she was sitting and talking with a friend. Hours later she died in a hospital emergency room as her father held her.

At the trial, Juan testified, beseeching the jury to offer leniency. He told them that he had forgiven the man who killed his daughter. The jury gave the man the most lenient sentence possible under law. The week before Christmas that year, Juan appeared at the front door of the convicted man's home bearing gifts for everyone in the family. As the man's wife opened the door cautiously, Juan smiled at her and said, "Merry Christmas." She couldn't believe this man's generosity, and many who hear this story cannot believe it as well. But it is every bit as true as the gospel that inspired it.

Dear God, inspire us to venture so far into forgiveness that we might leave all bitterness behind. Amen.

A Mare Named Jan

"Is not this the fast that I choose: to loose the bonds of wickedness, to undo the thongs of the yoke, to let the oppressed go free, and to break every yoke?" (Isaiah 58:6)

—⁓—

I rode Jan hard that long summer, and she was the most ornery horse I've ever attempted to befriend. She only understood spurs and a fine spade bit. Nothing else worked. She didn't want to collaborate with us on that Colorado ranch, but work was our purpose, and it fell to me to see that she did her part.

Every morning was the same. As I attempted to coax her out of a stall, she'd rear and kick. I always gave her room but never capitulated to her attempts at intimidation. Once she did settle down, I asked, "Are you finished?" She'd snort and rear one last time before I saddled her and rode her hard. Through the whole of the summer I felt for her. But there were chores to be done, and she and I would do them even if we had to fight.

On the last day of August, I rode her to a gate that opened into a meadow that was so expansive as to conceal from view the most distant fence. I gently removed her saddle and flung it into the bed of the pickup. Still holding her halter, I removed the bridle, and then slipped the rope off her head. She turned and ran like the wind until I could see her no longer. As I watched her disappear, I asked her to forgive me for taking from her the God-given gift of freedom during that long and difficult season we had shared.

We give thanks, Lord, that love is freedom. Amen.

Uncle Will

"And forgive us our debts, / As we also have forgiven our debtors."
(Matthew 6:12)

—∽—

Uncle Will peddled produce and fresh-laid eggs, sweet milk and buttermilk, and even some clabber in one of the poorest neighborhoods in all of the piney woods. Eighty-five years before I came into this world, these shacks formed the slave quarters of our small community, thus gaining the sobriquet "the Quarter." When I was a boy, most residents of the Quarter were illiterate, and all were desperately poor. Nevertheless, Uncle Will peddled in their midst by offering goods on credit. He kept his records in a spiral pocket notebook and never cheated a customer out of so much as a penny. On the day he died, I suspect every soul in the Quarter owed him some small amount of money. But if he worried about those debts, he never let on. On occasion, I would hear him say, "It's far better to forgive than to squeeze." And forgiveness is not only what he did; it is what his spirit so eloquently expressed. He forgave liberally and enjoyed life each day he lived it, and everyone who knew him recognized him as a man for whom forgiving seemed as easy as whistling for his cows in the evening.

O God, thank you for those who have come before us to show us how to become. Amen.

A Largemouth Bass

"Deliverance belongs to the LORD!" **(Jonah 2:9)**

—꿀—

I've been fishing for years, but only one time have I snagged a trophy. I realized that I had something on the end of the line that might be big enough to swallow a prophet fleeing to Tarshish. My rod bent forward, and the reel began to sing as if it had been trained for solos. "Oh, my," I whispered, as suddenly the monster surfaced to wag her head back and forth as though she was dissenting, which of course she was. I allowed her all the line she required and waited as patiently as a beekeeper. A second and a third time she jumped in protest, but all to no avail.

Minutes later she lay exhausted in the shallow water beneath my boots. I retrieved her gently and quickly weighed her. She came in at exactly twelve pounds. I removed the hook from her big upper lip, and then kissed her on her large green head and whispered, "I'm sorry I messed with you, sweet old lady. Now, go on home." With that I returned the grand fish to the waters she had made her home for likely more than a decade. The swish of her tail spoke a word of forgiveness that filled me with joy.

Thank you, Lord, that deliverance is always ours for the asking. Amen.

A Bear in the Night

Thou dost guide me with thy counsel, and afterward thou wilt receive me to glory. **(Psalm 73:24)**

—ᴍ—

I should never have done it, but I was young and filled with mischief. The night was dark, and the little girls and their pretty camp counselors had camped on the banks of the river not a hundred yards from a cabin I shared that summer with three other college seniors. An hour after the dark that comes late in the Colorado Rockies, I donned the bearskin and walked clumsily toward the girls' camp accompanied by my buddies. One growl was all that was required for the coeds and their charges to stir and fill the night with shrieks. I rolled in laughter and was proud of the prank until the next morning, when I was confronted by a group of women who informed me that I had ruined the weekend and terrified their young campers. "We'll never be able to get these girls to go into the woods again," one woman said. I told them I was sorry, but being sorry didn't suffice.

Today I regard that evening as a paradigm for what is often described as "harmless fun." I've learned this: If fun causes someone else pain, it's not harmless. I wish I could find those women today so that I might make amends. But I have no idea who they are, much less where they are. Still I know God forgives me, and never again will I pursue fun at someone else's expense. Receiving forgiveness brings with it the responsibility of learning.

Thank you, Lord, that wisdom may be derived from mistakes. Amen.

Surly Psychologist

Therefore, if any one is in Christ, he is a new creation; the old has passed away, behold, the new has come. (**2 Corinthians 5:17**)

———◊◊◊———

The psychologist who examined me three years prior to my ordination was surly, even abusive. Later I discovered that I was not the only candidate she had hurt. Others knew her as the "Cruel Doctor." At the time, I naively believed that those in the helping professions would be kind, but this woman quickly disabused me of such a notion. She was as hard as an anvil and as biting as a pack of puppies. Even before I settled down into the chair where I was to receive the results of the two days of testing, she barked, "Well, you're not nearly as smart as you think you are, sir." It was downhill after that.

Seventeen years later I attended a lecture she delivered. Following her talk, I approached her and told her that her treatment of me had been abusive. She smiled, reached out and took my hand, and asked, "Can you forgive me?" A bit taken aback, I said, "Well, I suppose forgiveness is what this faith is about." She responded, "I've kept up with you for years. You've done well. I was mean to you and to so many others. I regret that." I hugged her. No hug I've offered has ever felt better.

Lord, thank you that your grace can turn sour moments into wonderful memories. Amen.

A Table Warp

There is no fear in love, but perfect love casts out fear. (**1 John 4:18**)

—〰—

Fifty years after the War Between the States, my grandmother's family traveled to East Texas in a covered wagon. Among other things they brought with them was a handmade table that would serve them for decades. As a child, I sat at that table on two pillows in a chair, and, counter to my mother's admonitions, I placed my elbows on a warp in that table each time we bowed for grace. Above my head was a calendar of Jesus in the garden at Gethsemane and bearing the date 1949. (I was in the sixth grade before I realized that Jesus was not crucified in 1949.) Often I would place a full tumbler of fresh cow's milk on that warp. The result was always the same: disaster. Everyone at the table would jump up and do their best to stop the small river of milk. My brother would laugh, while my mother would sigh in disbelief that I'd done it again. I never meant to spill my milk, and often when I'd sit down, I'd make it a point to place my glass squarely on the level table. But then, once more, I'd forget the warp, and the tumbler would do exactly what it was made to do—tumble. My grandfather would soothe my shame by saying, "Bobby, we still love you."

Remind us that love is always bigger than our mistakes. Amen.

A Cry for Reconciliation

I will bless the Lord at all times; / his praise shall continually be in my mouth. **(Psalm 34:1)**

—ɰ—

A woman called to thank me for a newspaper column I'd written. She next described her futile attempt at a relationship with a daughter-in-law who wants nothing to do with her. She wonders how she has offended this younger woman. She searches her mind in the hope of finding some offensive part of herself that has alienated a woman she has only tried to love. To date, she has happened upon no answer.

I invited her to pray for her daughter-in-law, and to leave her attempt at reconciliation at that. She asked, "But what have I done wrong?" I responded, "Likely nothing. Often our relational problems are an external reflection of some conflict within our own troubled soul." I don't think she understood, because she insisted that the Bible teaches reconciliation. I concurred, but I added to the biblical mandate a simple invitation that she entrust to God the outcome of every relationship. Until her daughter-in-law becomes willing to be reconciled from within, she will likely not seek to be at peace with a woman who wants only harmony. Reconciliation begins with the prayer that the Spirit might heal us from the inside out.

Lord God, make us sufficiently whole to be entrusted with the ministry of reconciliation. Amen.

Solitary Confinement

I sought the LORD, and he answered me, / and delivered me from all my fears. (Psalm 34:4)

―◊―

Solitude is healing, but isolation is not. Solitude is voluntary, while isolation is punitive. These conditions may appear similar, but in reality they are as far apart as a shadow is from sunlight. The first can be a means for the discovery of love, whereas the second is a test of one's mettle. With isolation, terror lurks beneath that thin membrane separating willpower from exhaustion.

A man writes from a solitary cell in a North Texas jail, but he is not blessed by solitude. He reports that his problem is drugs. I disagree. His deeper problem is with fear, and his attempted solution is to palliate a chronic angst with chemicals. This never works, because, in theological terminology, he has attempted to replace his trust in the Spirit with a dependency upon something else. He writes today of the specific fear of not being forgiven by his family, and he asks for advice. My written suggestion is simple. First pray, and then write your heartfelt amends and mail them. Give the results to God, I tell him. I pray that he will now pray.

Father, open us so that we might finally discover the truth that we are made for love. Amen.

Surrender

"Nevertheless not my will, but thine, be done." (Luke 22:42b)

—ɯ—

Sometimes all we can do is surrender. This discipline comes under the rubric of giving up control of what it is we cannot control, and this includes all circumstances where we discover we are powerless.

During her adolescent years, my daughter taught me the spiritual power inherent in claiming my powerlessness. She decided that high school was not her cup of tea. Although she never actually dropped out, she slid so far toward the bottom of her class that it was difficult to imagine that she might have a future that included college. Guilt caused sleepless nights that generated a resentment eclipsing any hope, much less any real empathy. I was at a loss as to what to do. In anguish I cried out to the heavens on a winter day when the air was cold enough to turn my nose crimson. The silence that ensued mysteriously invited me to surrender her to the Virgin Mary. "I can't do that," I reflexively protested. "I'm a Protestant!" Nevertheless, I did just that, and five years later I cried tears of joy as I watched her graduate *magna cum laude* from a Catholic university on the High Holy Feast Day of the Blessed Mother.

Surrender invites grace, and grace will do the rest.

Holy God, grant us the courage to let go. Amen.

Without Words

We know that in everything God works for good with those who love him, who are called according to his purpose. (**Romans 8:28**)

—m—

Her boyfriend was cruel to her on the day they broke up. He spoke harsh words so as to justify his decision never to see her again. She wept, sought solace from friends, and in time got over it. In the parlance, she "moved on with her life" and developed new relationships.

Last night he called her to report that he had wrecked his motorcycle and was in dire need of her assistance. Even with all the pain he knew he'd caused, he guessed correctly that she would be the one most likely to respond to his cry. Not surprisingly, she stayed at the hospital with him until the physician pronounced him sufficiently fit to return to his work.

Grace is her way. She forgives liberally, and almost always without the encumbrance of words. Even when she easily could have said, "No way!" she showed up and did what love requires because her soul is good, and because she knows far better than most that this life is about expressing love. She is grace, and in her I often see "on earth as it is in heaven."

Father God, make me an instrument of love. Amen.

Mercy

"Blessed are the merciful, for they shall obtain mercy."
(Matthew 5:7)

───ɯ───

Mercy is at the center of all good spirituality. This is why Jesus teaches us in the Beatitudes that the merciful shall obtain mercy. Until we are merciful, we likely will remain self-absorbed and more than a little defensive. This is so because the opposite of mercy is not necessarily a disposition of harshness, but rather a strong investment in and attachment to the self of our own creation. Being immersed in this homemade identity is what the people in the Recovery Movement describe as being in bondage to one's self. This is the antithesis of mercy. Said another way, to be self-absorbed is to place one's interests above the expression of love, while to be merciful is to accept, forgive, and love first and foremost and to ask questions later.

Many years ago in Dallas I called an executive of a major department store and asked him if he'd be willing to give a man from the streets a job. His response was one of the most merciful I have ever heard. He said, "Sure, what does this fellow do?"

Lord, open our hearts to receive the mercy we so need to give away. Amen.

Lacy

So teach us to number our days / that we may get a heart of wisdom.
(Psalm 90:12)

—⋘—

Lacy called to report that his mother was dying and that he needed bus fare to Shreveport. I met him downtown, put up the money for his bus ticket, and waited with him until he boarded the bus. Before saying "So long," I handed him a twenty-dollar bill and said, "Lacy, this is a little food money. Take it." He feigned refusal, then grabbed the bill and stuffed it into his pocket. He grinned so wide his ears seemed to disappear.

Days later he returned to interrupt me. Put off by his intrusiveness, I managed to calm myself enough to invite him in to the office. "I'm busy," I announced. Then I thought to ask, "How is your mother?" Tears rolled down his ruddy cheeks. He said, "I lied to you. My mother died more than ten years ago. I tricked you so I could go to the horse races in Louisiana. I bet a hundred dollars on a horse and lost it all. I hitchhiked back, and I came here to ask your forgiveness." "I'll have to think about that some, Lacy," I said. "The forgiving part is easy, but it's the trusting part that's hard." Can there be forgiveness without trust? After much thought, I suppose so.

Teach us, O God, that erring on the side of compassion is right. Amen.

Florence

"But I say to you, Love your enemies and pray for those who perse-cute you." (Matthew 5:44)

—✲—

Florence grew up in poverty and today resides in its cruel midst. If she chose to, she could take her brother up on his offer to relocate her to his lake house in Wisconsin. But she stays put for the children of her neighborhood who come to her tiny house seven days a week because no one else wants them. She feeds, clothes, and teaches them with a spirit that appears undaunted by the challenge of never having enough of anything. Almost every evening, some down-on-his-luck drug dealer rattles the front gate, and she walks out of her front door and hands a hot meal over the fence. Not long ago she handed such a hot plate through the open gate only to have the recipient of her generosity unleash his attack dog. The wounds she suffered required a hundred and forty stitches to her face and a full week in the hospital. The first night she returned home, the same man with the same dog again rattled the gate, and Florence approached the fence, where she once more handed the man a full plate of food.

Lord, teach us to love with the tenacity of Florence. Amen.

Dignity

"For they all contributed out of their abundance; but she out of her poverty has put in everything she had, her whole living."
(Mark 12:44)

—∽∽—

For years I received an intriguing contribution to the soup kitchen on a monthly basis. There was no telephone number printed on the check, so I ventured forth one afternoon to locate the woman who sent our ministry two dollars a month. I found this donor's apartment, which was nothing more than a room or two carved out of what had once been a mansion.

I knocked on the door and waited. Moments later an elderly woman pulled open the door and smiled. I introduced myself, and she invited me in. I began, "Ma'am, I want you to know that we're grateful for your gift, but the truth is that the soup kitchen is doing just fine. So, if you could use the money for yourself, that would be fine with us." She said, "Mr. Lively, I give 10 percent of my Social Security check to the Lord; 8 percent goes to my church, and 2 percent goes to your soup kitchen. I appreciate your sensitivity, but please don't take from me my dignity." I rose from the chair and begged, "Ma'am, please forgive me." She smiled and said, "Oh, that's easy; you meant no harm."

Never have I been so humbled by the power of dignity.

Humble us, Father, so that we may learn humility. Amen.

Pancho

God was in Christ reconciling the world to Himself, not counting their trespasses against them. (2 Corinthians 5:19 NASB)

—∿∿—

Pancho, a border collie, was the best squirrel dog in the county. However, his bark summoned me too far one cold afternoon. I crossed our fence and followed his plaintive wails all the way up a creek bottom I'd never explored. The sun was slipping behind a veil of clouds intent upon blessing the piney woods with drizzle, but I could tell by the frequency in his hoarse voice that Pancho was onto a squirrel.

Arriving at the scene, I saw Pancho had so spooked that squirrel that I figured this little creature would not show himself again until the dogwoods bloomed. I did my best to talk that squirrel out of the hollow of that hickory, but all to no avail. Finally, I announced, "OK, Pancho, let's go home." Pancho bolted, abandoning me to the shadows. I was much too big to cry, and yet too scared not to. Just as a winter moon rose to cast a faint glow upon the cold woods, I heard my father whistle. I answered by firing my gun into the night. As we walked home together, my father draped his arm around my shoulder and said, "We all get lost from time to time." In his own quiet way he was forgiving me for trespassing. The grace he offered dripped into my soul one soothing drop at a time like warm honey over a raw throat.

Dear Lord, inspire us to forgive the errors we make, and even more the ones others make. Amen.

Payoff

Behold, how good and pleasant it is / when brothers dwell in unity!
(Psalm 133:1)

—⚭—

What's the payoff for hanging on to anger? What emotional dividends are derived from spectacular fantasies of vengeance? And what benefit can be found in obsessing about justice and fairness and the like? These are good questions, and the only real answer to each is contained in this one word: *zero*! Simply put, resentment is always a zero-sum game. No one ever wins with resentment, and nothing is to be gained by it. So why do we hold on to resentments? The answer is simple: Constructing resentments is as natural as sneezing in allergy season. Moreover, it's the sad and, over time, even debilitating product of every life dedicated to self-preoccupation. This is so because the self-centered mind is determined to win and/or get even.

But a soul so stretched by suffering as to be made malleable sometimes opens itself to the healing properties of grace. Once this great, although subtle, power enters the equation, nothing remains the same as the disheartening sum of zero gives way quickly to one blessing after the other. First joy is added, and then comes serenity. Reconciliation follows, and this shepherds a soul toward greater and greater intimacy with God. Resentment is always a locked door, while grace remains the key to happiness.

Heavenly Father, help us find the key to happiness. Amen.

33

Old, Sweet Nellie

But the fruit of the Spirit is love, joy, peace, patience, kindness, good-ness, faithfulness, gentleness, self-control; against such there is no law. (Galatians 5:22-23)

—⚡—

Nellie was Uncle Carl's dog, but she came to live on the farm because the family judged she'd be happy herding cows and chasing a rooster whenever the mood struck. Evidence pointed to the fact that this was a good decision, because Nellie consistent-ly appeared happy. Whether she was paddling in the stock tank or lying contentedly at my feet as I shelled purple hull peas on the front porch, she was the emblem of inner peace.

One evening as we sat on the porch, Uncle Will pointed and said, "Look at old, sweet Nellie." (Any time he spoke of her, he enjoyed assigning to her the descriptors *old* and *sweet*.) "Look at the old, sweet dog wagging her tail."

Nellie sensed she had become the focus of our attention, hence her tail wagging increased. Uncle Will continued, "Her tail is pure hap-piness, while the rest of her is love." For the first time, I made the connection. All real happiness is born of the willingness to love.

Decades later, I would make another equally important discovery: Forgiveness is the bedrock of the spirituality that makes love possi-ble. Where forgiveness is not at the foundation of faith, what will be expressed will be so superficial that no real happiness can take root.

God, make forgiveness the foundation of our faith. Amen.

Amazing Grace

From now on, therefore, we regard no one from a human point of view; even though we once regarded Christ from a human point of view, we regard him thus no longer. (2 Corinthians 5:16)

—〰—

Ordinarily the governing body of the church that reared me would sing the doxology after each examination of a young man or young woman who appeared before them with the idea of becoming a candidate for the ministry. I came before this body on February 16, 1969, with the humble request that they take me under their wing and sponsor me as a candidate as I negotiated the waters of theological education and, later, the rigors required for ordination. They posed a few questions, and as best I could tell, they appeared not unduly ruffled by my responses. One man did remember, however, that as a boy I had earned a widely held reputation for mischief. I couldn't dispute his recollection because the evidence supported his claim. A hush fell over this august body before I responded, "Mea culpa, sir." He smiled and said, "Our custom is to stand and sing the doxology once we confirm a candidate for the ministry. However, in the case of this young man, I recommend that we approve him and stand and sing " 'Amazing Grace.' " And that is what they did.

Holy Father, thank you that grace can transform the soul. Amen.

Mannequin Slaughter

The fear of the LORD is the beginning of knowledge; / fools despise wisdom and instruction. (Proverbs 1:7)

—∿∿—

The temptation proved too great once we spied the mannequin's feet sticking out of a Dumpster. We were sixteen, the night was waning, and the top was down on my buddy's father's convertible, so what else could we do? We hauled the pasteboard man to church, where with a key we were not authorized to possess we opened the door to the room where donated clothes were stored. We searched until we found a business suit that didn't fit, along with a pair of scuffed shoes, a dress shirt, a tie, and even a hat. Moments later, with our now dapper mannequin in tow, we headed for the bright lights of downtown. We paused on the river bridge only long enough to throw him over the rail. A policeman we never saw flipped on red rotating lights, and for the next several hours both my buddy and I sat in jail.

Before the sun could rise, a gruff, but wise, sergeant appeared at our cell door and said, "Boys, we located your victim. Now, I recommend that you go home and never do anything like this again." I took the man's advice, and every time I pass over any river I am reminded of grace.

Lord God, our Father, thank you that grace leads us home. Amen.

The Power of Faith

Live by the Spirit, I say, and do not gratify the desires of the flesh.
(Galatians 5:16 NRSV)

—ɯɯ—

Kierkegaard said that faith wills the downfall of reason. This makes sense, because it is not good for one's image to hold a faith that requires of us to forgive liberally. After all, who wants to be viewed as a pushover? Reason, then, is the refined product of the mind's best efforts, yet it is guided always by the culture that shapes it. Reason seeks to be viewed as respectable and is keenly conscious of, if not obsessed with, its reputation. Its nature is to advance a concept of justice that is not at all dissimilar from vengeance. Further, reason enjoys being right and will strive to prove its point and to justify its behavior with what else but reason.

Grace, however, is more concerned about love than it is about being reasonable, and it transcends the culture by rejecting every thought of retribution. The Spirit appears out of place in a dog-eat-dog world that is run on reason. This is not surprising, because God is Spirit, and this forgiving Mystery invites us to be in the world but never of it.

God, give us the courage to live by a faith that transcends even reason. Amen.

International Bridge

"For I was hungry and you gave me food, I was thirsty and you gave me drink." (Matthew 25:35)

—◊◊◊—

It's commonly known as the International Bridge. Perhaps a more appropriate appellation might be the Bridge of Contrasts, because it joins two nations, one rich and the other desperately poor. These two nations bump up against each other in a way that happens nowhere else. Here, the first world meets the third world, and the rich nation invests billions of dollars protecting itself from the other's desperation. One nation is Lazarus, who in Luke's Gospel lies at the gate of the rich man. And the other nation is the rich man, who is indifferent to Lazarus's suffering.

As I walked across the International Bridge, I encountered a little girl who could not have been more than three years of age. Her tiny hand was outstretched and empty, and I glimpsed her only long enough to intuit the obvious toll required by the grinding poverty into which she was born. I did not dare look at her for long, because to do so would be to risk seeing Jesus, and his holy countenance would require I become involved, perhaps even committed. So I passed her by and asked God to forgive me.

Wherever poverty exists, indifference lurks. Forgiveness is the beginning of the solution.

Father, forgive our indifference. Amen.

Inside Job

And one does not take the honor upon himself, but he is called by God, just as Aaron was. **(Hebrews 5:4)**

—∭—

Grace begins at home. Hence, the power of forgiveness is launched with the willingness to forgive oneself. Until we are able to accept God's grace, we will not be able to offer it. This is why Jesus tells us that the merciful obtain mercy. Simply put, what we search for eventually finds us.

This is why my friend Harry is such a miracle. For the first half of his life he searched only for that next bottle of two-dollar wine, which he used to numb his pain for a few hours each evening as he sat under a Dallas bridge and cursed God and his life in that order. One memorable morning, I dragged him out from under the foundation of a derelict building in downtown Dallas, where he had gone to drink himself to death. On that day he cursed me. Later, Harry not only recovered from a near-lethal dose of alcohol and pneumonia, he also surrendered to God the habit of his self-loathing. Today he serves as a seminary-trained ordained clergyman. As I see it, the real miracle in this man's transformation is that he asked God's forgiveness, and the answer to that simple prayer was one of the greatest miracles I've been privileged to witness.

Lord, thank you that grace heals. Amen.

Where to Begin

He restores my soul. **(Psalm 23:3a)**

—◊—

He rests in a hospital bed as he asks me where to begin his experience with the mystery we call grace. His life is in jeopardy due to decades of abusing alcohol. He realizes that he has ravaged his body, perhaps irreparably. But even as he trembles on the threshold of death's shadowed valley, he inquires what it means to ask God to restore one's soul.

"Can you forgive yourself for the damage you've done to your body?" I ask.

"With help, I can," he responds weakly, with tears coursing down both cheeks. "If God will only strengthen me to do that, I will in time forgive myself," he whispers as his bottom lip trembles.

"Restoration begins always with forgiveness," I say, as he nods.

"Why is that?" he asks in a whisper.

"Because mercy is all there is."

Appearing puzzled, he asks, "And why is that?"

I say, "Because mercy is who God is."

His smile speaks for his soul.

Holy Spirit, open our closed minds to the mystery of it all. Amen.

True Freedom

For freedom Christ has set us free. Stand firm, therefore, and do not submit again to a yoke of slavery. **(Galatians 5:1 NRSV)**

—ıᴍ—

As an adolescent, I was convinced that freedom was hedonism. To be free meant to be able to seek any kind of pleasure whenever I wanted. By the time I finished seminary, I had changed my mind and had become convinced that true freedom meant to be obedient to God. This idea served me well for almost three decades until I discovered firsthand the amazing, even transforming, power inherent in forgiveness. As I see it today, we are only free once we decide to forgive whatever and whoever stands in need of forgiveness. If we cannot bring ourselves to forgive, we remain in bondage. Transformation begins with the acceptance of a grace so radical and so life-changing that it liberates us from the need to hold a grudge or the habit of being right or any concern for retributive justice. Forgiveness liberates us from the self we made up so that we might become who it is God created us to be.

Liberate us, Lord, from every consideration of retribution. Amen.

A Healing Exercise

Heal me, O LORD, and I shall be healed. **(Jeremiah 17:14)**

—∿—

A friend tells me that she discovered God in her rage. Her wealthy husband had betrayed her and then abandoned her to care for three children he apparently cared little about. For years she seethed, until hypertension became a threat to her health if not her life. After a diagnosis that rattled her, she visited a city park to sit alone on a bench and to attempt the first prayer she had offered in the years since the day her husband abandoned her. This friend claims that inspiration appeared to her in the form of a pigeon that proclaimed to her a message of forgiveness. As she studied this bird strutting in small circles beneath her feet, she happened upon an invitation that came to her mind from somewhere deep within. This gentle voice invited her to give up going around in circles and to begin a journey toward God. Humbly, she asked, "How?" The voice invited her to pray for her ex-husband every morning and every night for a full month, beseeching the Holy Spirit to bless him with health and goodness. Courageously, my friend accepted this invitation, and within two months her doctor informed her that her overall health had improved dramatically.

O Lord, lead us out of our obsessions. Amen.

What I Didn't Say

And the tongue is a fire. (**James 3:6**)

―――

When I was a boy, my grandfather would say, "Bobby, sometimes you talk too much with your mouth." He was dead right. I was blessed with a tongue to speak, and like most people, I misused it before I realized that the hurtful words I spoke had gone forth to do their damage. Today, I've learned to rein in those ugly expressions that so desperately long to attach themselves to the all too frequent cataracts of unkind thoughts. In fact, each time I enter a meeting or any serious conversation, I write the following old Jewish proverb on a piece of paper where my eyes can read these words: "I've never had to repent for what I didn't say." *Not* saying what I sometimes want to say and speaking instead the truth of God's love is a much healthier and far more peaceful way to live. The more I am silent and thoughtful, the less I find I need to ask for forgiveness.

Father, bless us with the gift of restraint. Amen.

The Otherness of God

Yet thou hast made him little less than God. **(Psalm 8:5)**

—∿∿—

God is that pure otherness we know as holiness. We are all made of the same stuff, earth enlivened by the divine breath. Regardless of race, ethnicity, nationality, or skin color, earth and divine breath are what compose us. Hence, we are all unique and very complex expressions of the same generative Spirit. This is the ancient Hebrew perspective. From the New Testament view we learn that we are potential awaiting the Spirit to birth us a second time into a whole new creation. The writer of Genesis views us as created reflections of the Creator, while a psalmist once characterized us as just less than God and crowned with glory and honor. Jesus assures us that we can even evolve spiritually into sons and daughters of God. The holiness of our origin and the promise of God's abiding love should inform us of our inestimable value. How strange it is then that most of us think of ourselves as unworthy. The world we live in is often a cruel teacher and too frequently also a purveyor of lies. Nevertheless, we have been made in the image of love. God, forgive us when we act in ways that belie this great truth.

O God, forgive us for the falsehoods we embrace. Amen.

Those Other Boys

O God, thou knowest my folly; / the wrongs I have done are not hidden from thee. (Psalm 69:5)

—⚏—

Summer was fast drawing to a close, and sixth grade loomed on September's horizon. There was little to do but wait upon the advent of another Labor Day. Only because boredom can be the fuse that sometimes ignites war, I ventured to the end of the street, where I was taunted by a group of boys I'd known since the first grade. At school, we were classmates and even friends. During the summer months, however, we viewed one another as enemies only because we lived at opposite ends of the street. From September through May we called each other by our first names, but in the summer we used other monikers. I returned their taunts with threats.

The next evening I returned with some boys from my end of the street, where we chucked horse apples at the other boys and they at us. Suddenly a glass windowpane shattered, and we scattered like roaches in daylight. Within mere seconds, the street was filled with concerned parents. An hour later all of us stood before the woman whose window our horse-apple war had destroyed, and one of the boys begged for forgiveness. For the next two months my weekly allowance of fifty cents was set aside to pay for that window. Only after it was paid for did the woman tell us that she forgave us. I don't think I've ever been more grateful to hear those words.

Teach us, Lord, of the senselessness of enemies. Amen.

Playing Games with Chickens

But let justice roll down like waters, / and righteousness like an ever-flowing stream. (Amos 5:24)

—ɯ—

One evening I was struck with the novel idea of playing the board game Monopoly with my grandmother's chickens. I dumped a whole bucket of feed into one pen, where maybe six or seven hens devoured a mound that resembled a miniature Pike's Peak. "You live on Boardwalk," I announced to those fortunate and fat old hens as I referred to the premier property on the Monopoly board. I then tossed a few pellets to the large flock of incredulous birds that could not figure out how to make their way into the Boardwalk pen. "And the rest of you chickens live on Mediterranean Avenue," I announced, loud enough for my grandfather to hear. Seeing my cruel mischief, he commanded me to redistribute the food and to make amends to the entire flock. I shoveled the mound of chicken feed over the fence and in the direction of the hungry birds, but I could not figure out exactly how to right the wrong I had done. Finally, I decided that redistribution was apology enough, and I left it at that.

Teach us, Holy God, that justice is love spread all around. Amen.

Hollow Prayers

Likewise the Spirit helps us in our weakness; for we do not know how to pray as we ought, but the Spirit himself intercedes for us with sighs too deep for words. (Romans 8:26)

—m—

While I regard confession as important, even fundamental, to faith development, I have never found much comfort in the corporate prayers I've recited for a lifetime that beseech God to forgive me for my sins of commission and omission. Like most folks, I traffic in both kinds of sin. I omit, and I also commit. Nevertheless, to keep the expression of my sins generic does me no good whatsoever. In fact, I wonder if this practice does not allow me to avoid God by bringing before the throne of grace nothing more than generalities. Not surprisingly, I tend to view all generic confessions as hollow, if not a waste of God's time and ours. My confession becomes efficacious only when I choose to be rigorously honest with God and share what's on my mind about how it is I've often fallen short. Once I make an honest confession of my sins, I feel better, because the grace arrives to wash over me like waters of baptism. But if my prayer remains hollow, nothing will really happen. The distance between honest and hollow prayer, it seems, is the same distance that separates a fired bullet from a smoky blank.

Father in heaven, we do not pray as we ought. Amen.

What to Do with Enemies

Do you not know that friendship with the world is enmity with God?
(James 4:4)

—∿—

The Psalter is packed with references to people having enemies, and what harsh treatment the ancient poets hope God will mete out against those who have done them wrong. This is interesting theology, but from the point of understanding that all human thought, even our most inspired thoughts about God, is always a work in progress. The idea of vengeance is counter to everything Jesus proclaimed. One thousand years after the psalms were written, God's view regarding the issue of enemies is revealed in Christ's teachings in his Sermon on the Mount: "You have heard that it was said, 'You shall love your neighbor and hate your enemy.' But I say to you, Love your enemies and pray for those who persecute you, so that you may be children of your Father in heaven; for he makes his sun rise on the evil and the good, and sends rain on the righteous and on the unrighteous" (Matthew 5:43-45 NRSV).

Once we pray for an enemy, we will no longer have an enemy. It's that simple. Hence, the only real victory one may experience in the context of human conflict is to petition God on behalf of one's enemy, while it is always a great tragedy to harbor any desire to get even. Nothing I know can make us more miserable than the foolish conviction that vengeance serves God.

Liberate us, O Lord, from vengeance. Amen.

Democracy and Grace

Now as they were eating, Jesus took bread, and blessed, and broke it, and gave it to the disciples and said, "Take, eat; this is my body." (Matthew 26:26)

—〰—

A learned friend believes that the two most democratic gatherings on the planet are a Willie Nelson concert and the Lord's Table. Inclusion is always God's way, and any place where all people are welcome, regardless of who they are or what they've done or not done, is where I also belong. In fact, each time I approach the Communion rail or someone brings a tray of wafers and cups to the pew, I know for certain that I am absolutely forgiven. I did nothing to earn this gift, and God knows I don't deserve it. I cannot be good enough to win its reward, and nothing I can do or not do is bad enough to take it away. When it comes to grace, I am always desperately in need, and I've yet to meet a human being who is not. Grace is what we require most as mistake-making human beings, and our need for it is the great leveler.

Thank you, God, that grace is never cheap but always ours for the asking. Amen.

Negative Voices

... and after the earthquake a fire, but the LORD was not in the fire; and after the fire a still small voice. (**1 Kings 19:12**)

—∿—

How do we not hear the voices in our heads that shame us and so ruthlessly ridicule our most precious dreams? This is a good question, and one I've been asked often over three decades of listening to the yearnings of many hearts. The best answer I know to offer is to suggest that we cannot *not* listen. The voices are there, yet they speak to us only in half-truths and full-blown falsehoods. What they tell us is most often not even close to reality, yet the messages they proclaim are always harsh, loud, cruel, belittling, and most of all persistent. So what do we do?

The solution is simple: We pray. As Mark Twain put it, we cannot pray a lie. Consequently, when we pray—and by that I mean really listen to God—in time we will hear love whisper to us in the silence. And what will it say? It will convince us without words that we are accepted just as we are. Once we hear this, we can then forgive the voices for showing up and lying to us with such frequency and such relentlessness. With sufficient practice in the art of listening to God, the voices will fade, and their power will diminish.

Lord God, make us ready to hear the truth. Amen.

Passivity

"You have seen what I did to the Egyptians, and how I bore you on eagles' wings and brought you to myself." (Exodus 19:4)

—⁓—

Passivity is not at all the same thing as forgiveness, although many people confuse doing nothing with grace. Passivity is an emotional, and for the most part unconscious, reaction to some perceived threat or to some great wrong that inflicts injury. Out of fear, the one who is hurt or abused may be prone to believing that forgiveness means ignoring the wrong or attempting to believe that no injury actually occurred. This is denial, not grace. Denial is always an unhealthy reaction to the fear of facing reality, while grace is the willingness to accept reality and then forgive. Denial is humanity's primary ego defense, while grace is God's great blessing given to empower us to love in a way that over time transforms a soul. Defense mechanisms keep us stuck, while grace liberates. Every expression of grace signals the truth that one has become dedicated to reality and is now willing to live within the bounds of God's will, while every demonstration of denial means that we have rejected grace and the clarity it promises. Denial always limits, while grace only liberates.

Dear Lord, grant us the courage to do whatever is required to pursue the truth. Amen.

Advice

The hearing ear and the seeing eye, / the LORD has made them both.
(Proverbs 20:12)

—⟶⟶⟶—

The first commandment of pastoral counseling is this: *Thou shall not give advice.* As well-intentioned human beings, we are tempted to believe that we can best love others by giving them our very best advice. Job's three friends, Bildad, Zophar, and Eliphaz, did just that. They thought that the best they could do for their suffering friend was to offer him advice. So one by one they showed up on his doorstep with what they held to be the answer to the genesis of his suffering. They meant well, but then advice-givers always do. There was only one problem with these righteous, God-fearing, credible, and very reasonable men: They were dead wrong! Fortunately, Job searched beyond their advice so that he might discover the truth that talking about God is not nearly so helpful as actually talking to God.

Much of the advice we have been given by well-intentioned people is also wrong. God so structured reality that all truth must necessarily be discovered. Although some advice is good and helpful, we must discipline ourselves to forgive those who once sought to set us straight, so that we may come to discover the greatest truth of all, which is that God accepts us no matter what poor advice we may have received and long ago lived by.

Lord God, place our feet on the path. Amen.

Bitterness Is Hazardous to Our Health

Jesus said to [Peter], "I do not say to you seven times, but seventy times seven." (Matthew 18:22)

—⟋⟍—

People tell me that they can't forgive, and this is never true. What is true is that they don't wish to forgive. By making the conscious decision not to forgive, we run the risk of elevating our blood pressure, taxing our cardiovascular system, suppressing our immune system, radically changing the hormonal balance in our bodies, and risking a serious affective disorder such as the onset of a major depression. The risks of bitterness are far too great for many of us to long consider carrying it around. In fact, it is toxic to the soul. I've never smoked, but after more than three decades of listening to other people, I have come to believe that it is less hazardous to our health to smoke a pack of cigarettes a day than to hang on to anger, resentment, and rage.

Depression occurs for many complex reasons, with perhaps the most common being repressed anger. Honest confession brings emotional toxins to the surface the way a rainy night coaxes night crawlers out of the soil deep below. Following confession, forgiveness ushers in the healing power of grace. Jesus is always for us, and he knows that our health is linked to forgiveness.

Grant us, O Lord, the wisdom to forgive. Amen.

The World's Greatest Fear

Do not be overcome by evil, but overcome evil with good.
(Romans 12:21)

—∞—

This world rejects reconciliation. Why? The reasons are many and complex, but suffice it to say that most people's lives are unconsciously guided by a tenacious and tyrannical little ego that is conditioned to equate success with winning and with being right. This is why revenge feels more natural than does forgiveness. But one of the great secrets of the universe is that grace is the truth, while thoughts of vengeance are always illusory, because they emanate from an identity we made up, as opposed to the self who was created in the divine image. Consequently, to seek reconciliation over other motives is to risk dying to all we know, and this idea terrifies us to the point of turning us away from God so that we can pretend that Christianity is a system of quaint beliefs that allow us to do life on our terms. Reconciliation is love and therefore always of God, while resentment is an expression of a fear that kills first the spirit and later the body. This is why Confucius said, "If you devote your life to seeking revenge, first dig two graves."

Holy Father, inspire in us the courage to love in spite of ourselves. Amen.

Casey

Save me, O God! / For the waters have come up to my neck.
(Psalm 69:1)

—m—

Casey would be near thirty today had he lived, and likely he'd be married and helping his father operate the family's sprawling horse ranch. But such a happy future was not to be his, because exactly one week after I met this tow-headed eight-year-old, he was murdered, along with his young mother. The assailant was not apprehended for more than a year, but it required much more time than a mere twelve months for the community of which he and his mother were a part to recover from the devastation wrought by wanton violence.

I met Casey and his mother in the cramped narthex of the Presbyterian church where I had preached that morning, only seven days before their deaths. I remember little about him except that his hair was so blond as to resemble cotton, and that his eyes held the promise of more adventure than one little boy could possibly enjoy in ten summers. The week following my introduction to Casey and his mom, their pastor called to report the horror. Stunned, I hung up the phone and stared at the wall, not knowing what to feel. Weeks later the pastor called again to report that he knew he must forgive, but he could not find it in himself to do so. I listened and responded only with the promise of prayer. Months later the pastor wrote to say that he had finally mustered the courage to ask God to help him forgive a killer still at large, and that for the first time in a long time he had slept through the night.

Lord, hear us when we say that forgiveness is sometimes so difficult. Amen.

God Needs No Forgiveness

"For as the rain and the snow come down from heaven, / and return not thither but water the earth, / making it bring forth and sprout, / giving seed to the sower and bread to the eater, / so shall my word be that goes forth from my mouth." **(Isaiah 55:10-11a)**

—⁘—

As a ten-year-old, I asked my grandmother if she thought God needed forgiving for inflicting upon us a seven-year drought. Some of our fence neighbors had gone broke, and during those seven long years, several folks, including even the brush arbor preachers, speculated that we must have done something to rile God. Why else would we be so punished with a sky that refused to cloud up, much less bless us with so much as a drop of rain?

I didn't know much about God, and what little Bible I'd read had been a condensed version intended for children; nevertheless, I couldn't make myself believe that we were being punished. In fact, I persuaded myself that it was God, and not us, who bore the lion's share of the responsibility for our misery. Consequently, one summer evening while on the front porch with my grandparents, I asked my grandmother if God might need for us to forgive him. My wise grandmother was rendered speechless by this presumptuous question, but my granddaddy smiled and kept on shelling the purple hull peas and said, "Son, God don't never need no forgiving. It's like this: It rains on the just and on the unjust, and someday, it will rain on us."

Father, forgive our foolishness. Amen.

A Pine Tree and a Process

For by grace you have been saved through faith; and this is not your own doing, it is the gift of God. **(Ephesians 2:8)**

—⟋⟍—

When I was very young, I heard lightning strike a distant lodgepole pine on a mountainside. I cautiously followed the tell-tale smoke until I happened upon a still smoldering stump. Unlike the bush in the story of Moses, the tree I happened upon was totally consumed by fire. Limbs weighing hundreds of pounds were thrown yards from the tree as though they were mere matchsticks. I will never forget the sight, and for the past half-century I've heard Christians describe the experience of sudden conversion in much the same way that lightning struck that tree. In fact, they speak of being "struck" by grace, which is a good way to view what theologian Paul Tillich called the moment when one accepts God's acceptance.

However, grace, or God's forgiveness, never stops with one bold, devastating, life-changing strike. While conversion may begin this way, the mystery that is grace is like a gentle, but relentless, pounding of waves against a sandy beach. It knows no beginning and has no end. It just is, yet simultaneously it changes forever all that it touches. Hence, grace begins with an event but never stops, as it invites us to collaborate with its power in that mysterious process the Bible calls salvation.

Open our hearts and our minds, O Father, so that we might collaborate with grace. Amen.

The Mystery of the Lord's Supper

Who can say, "I have made my heart clean; / I am pure from my sin"? (**Proverbs 20:9**)

—⁓—

A friend once opined, "It must be a real privilege to serve Communion to people." I don't remember how I responded to this man's unexpected observation, but I did pause long enough to ponder three questions: Is it a privilege? Is it an honor? Or is it much more?

After some thought, I have come to believe that the invitation to participate in the sacrament of Communion, or what many call the Lord's Supper, transcends even the categories of supposed privilege and honor. Nothing I have done or might do could make me worthy to offer the words of institution and then break the bread and pour out the wine in the holy name of Jesus. Even on my best days, I cannot be good enough to be judged by God worthy to function as a leader in this holy experience.

But thank God, being good enough is not the issue with God—grace is. For only by grace are we invited to taste and ingest the transforming power of forgiveness whether we lead in the offering of the sacrament or approach the rail to receive it with an open and grateful heart.

Thank you, Lord God, that our sin in no way makes you quit loving us. Amen.

Catching Up

I have swept away your transgressions like a cloud, / and your sins like mist; / return to me, for I have redeemed you. **(Isaiah 44:22)**

—◊—

The prophet we know as (Second) Isaiah warns against idols. Six centuries before the birth of Jesus, he wrote: "All who make idols are nothing, and the things they delight in do not profit; their witnesses neither see nor know, that they may be put to shame" (Isaiah 44:9). These words are given to us as a gift, yet too often we ignore them while we drive ourselves to search for salvation in anything but God's will. We may go to church and pray often, but for as long as we chase after the idols of status, money, and gadgets, we set ourselves up for a fall by constructing a life that is in service to the self while giving the praise to God. This never works, but we can't know this until our best efforts at happiness finally fail us, or in the words of the prophet, we are "put to shame."

Falling apart is not such a bad thing. In fact, it can be a very redemptive experience, because every defeat brings with it the possibility of turning to God where, if we are wise, we will ask to be forgiven. Once I heard a lecturer say, "Modern psychiatry is very close to catching up with the Old Testament." Today I understand the lecturer's meaning.

Keep us from the fascination with idols, Lord. Amen.

Letting Go

God is our refuge and strength, / a very present help in trouble.
(Psalm 46:1)

—⁓—

Any practitioner of a 12-step recovery program has heard the admonition to "let go and let God." I find it interesting how simple this sounds, but how difficult it is to pull off. Our nature tempts us to equate the ego's agenda with God's will. And because the culture teaches us to think this way, we are reluctant to relinquish the power we have invested the whole of our lives garnering and imposing. Because we view ourselves as in control, we don't want to let go, and we do want to be God.

Not long ago, I was visiting with a physician friend who was fretting over the condition of a particular patient. She said somewhat angrily, "I can do nothing more for this patient." I asked, "Can you give this person to God?" With eyes ablaze, she retorted angrily, "But what if God doesn't know what she's doing?" We both laughed immediately, and she said, "God, forgive me!" Playing along, I answered, "I suspect she does."

Lord God, make us wise enough to seek humility in all things. Amen.

Embarrassed by Anger

Do nothing from selfishness or conceit, but in humility count others better than yourselves. **(Philippians 2:3)**

—⚬—

I am embarrassed to confess that I once clung to bitterness as if it were hope. After ten years of serving a church as a pastor, I respectfully requested a three-month sabbatical so I could write. I was denied the request, and I resigned in protest. In retrospect, I see that the elders who denied my request were insensitive; but even more, I was immature. Unfortunately, my immaturity was far greater than their callosity. I pouted for years until, finally, I came to see that their decision had been a blessing. Unbeknownst to them and to me, God had transformed their decision into a great opportunity for growth. Years after the fact, I discovered that if I did not pray for the strength necessary to forgive these people, like Job I would find myself on the ash heap and scratching the boils of old and infected anger. Only by grace was I able to surrender the deep hurt that fueled the resentment. Once I did that, I was free to follow Jesus into a new life of expressing love. Anger was my sin, and I clung to it until finally I became willing to trust. This is not surprising, because trust is always the seed of salvation.

Plant in us the seed of trust, O God. Amen.

Needing Less

Indeed I count everything as loss because of the surpassing worth of knowing Christ Jesus my Lord. **(Philippians 3:8)**

—⚹—

I happened upon a bumper sticker recently that made me think about how spiritual truths can be far easier to consider than to live. The sticker attached to the rusty bumper of a pickup read: *The more you know, the less you need.*

I pondered this idea long enough to decide that it contained more truth than I was willing to let into my soul all at once, lest I be required to do the hard work required of all new commitments to holiness. But the more I think upon these words, the more I believe them to be true, because the more I know about forgiveness, and the more I experience God's gentle grace, the less I need to be right, or to be angry, or to harbor resentments, or to speak ill of brothers and sisters, or to waste time composing speeches I will never deliver. More of God is less of everything else. The greater the awareness of grace, the less the internal turmoil; and the greater the willingness to forgive, the less the misery generated by devotion to ourselves.

Make us aware, O Lord, and teach us so that we might grow. Amen.

Bakery Wall Wisdom

In him we have redemption through his blood, the forgiveness of our trespasses, according to the riches of his grace which he lavished upon us. **(Ephesians 1:7)**

—⁓—

Affixed to the wall of a small bakery in Fredericksburg, Texas, hangs this quotation: "It is not the moments we breathe that matter, but rather those moments that take from us our breath." I heartily agree. And every time I happen into a seemingly ordinary human being who by grace has been made extraordinary through the commitment to forgiveness, my breath is taken from me. I once thought that a magnificent mountain range at first light, or an exquisite desert rainbow, or wave upon wave of salt water crashing against a rocky coast at sunset would fill me with awe like nothing else could. But about that and so many other things, I was mistaken. While nature can be spectacular, only grace is transformative. And the fact is that there is nothing so breathtaking as a soul who has so completely accepted grace as to be able to express its essence.

Open our eyes, O Lord, to the wonder of grace. Amen.

Taking On the Big Hurts

I press on toward the goal for the prize of the upward call of God in Christ Jesus. **(Philippians 3:14)**

—⟋⟍—

I doubt any of us can forgive the big hurts without help. In fact, I suspect that such a spiritual feat requires more strength than any soul can muster without guidance and inspiration. Prodigious forgiveness is akin to mountain climbing. Before the onset of heart disease, I climbed the highest peak in Texas, which is not high, but does take its toll by offering the adventurous a very steep trail. Halfway up that mountain, with twenty or so folks behind me, I realized that likely this attempt was a mistake. Two-thirds of the way up, I realized I was in trouble. That's when the clouds finally lifted, and I discovered I was not two-thirds of the way up; I was still less than halfway. Pride mixed with a stout determination, and I prayed as I put one step in front of the other. Two hours later, I was on the summit, where I could see clearly 360 degrees.

This is always the way it is with forgiveness. Hard work, doubt, fear, pain, and frustration always precede clarity. I prayed my way up, and I also have learned to pray my way into forgiving those whom I must forgive. Once on the summit of that mountain I wrote in the register these words from the apostle Paul: "I press on toward the goal for the prize of the upward call of God in Christ Jesus" (Philippians 3:14).

Father, strengthen us to forgive even when it seems impossible. Amen.